TABLE OF CONTENTS

DISCLAIMER AND TERMS OF USE AGREEMENT:

Introduction

Your Own Personal Bailout

A Gift from the Government…NOT!

'Blank Checks'

Weekly Cash from a 24-Hour Window of Disruption

Skimming the Establishment

Cashing In

   Things You'll Need

Supporting Resources

Setting it Up!

The Claim Process

Making the Calls

Rehearsals

Records

I Have a Special Gift for My Readers

Meet the Author

Applied Income Model
Make Money from Homes Using This Very Simple Program
©Copyright 2012 by Dr. Leland Benton

DISCLAIMER AND TERMS OF USE AGREEMENT:

(Please Read This Before Using This Book)
This information is for educational and informational purposes only. The content is not intended to be a substitute for any professional advice, diagnosis, or treatment.
The authors and publisher of this book and the accompanying materials have used their best efforts in preparing this book.
The authors and publisher make no representation or warranties with respect to the accuracy, applicability, fitness, or completeness of the contents of this book. The information contained in this book is strictly for educational purposes. Therefore, if you wish to apply

ideas contained in this book, you are taking full responsibility for your actions.

The authors and publisher disclaim any warranties (express or implied), merchantability, or fitness for any particular purpose. The author and publisher shall in no event be held liable to any party for any direct, indirect, punitive, special, incidental or other consequential damages arising directly or indirectly from any use of this material, which is provided "as is", and without warranties. As always, the advice of a competent legal, tax, accounting, medical or other professional should be sought where applicable.

The authors and publisher do not warrant the performance, effectiveness or applicability of any sites listed or linked to in this book. All links are for information purposes only and are not warranted for content, accuracy or any other implied or explicit purpose. No part of this may be copied, or changed in any format, or used in any way other than what is outlined within this course under any circumstances. Violators will be prosecuted.

This book is © Copyrighted by ePubWealth.com.

Introduction

Welcome to Applied Income Model. I'm a regular ol' investor and to make things perfectly clear and upfront, I am no financial "guru" or wizard. I am a behavioral scientist trying to do exactly what you are trying to do; take care of my family and provide for my retirement until God calls me home. In my attempts to invest prudently and learn how to be a good money manager, I have seen some really "weird" things going on in terms of the areas of investment that are open to investors that tend to manage their own portfolios. I learned early on that I cannot compete with the big boys but I can invest in certain specialty "niche" markets that have little or no competition and the Applied Income Model is one such niche market. You are really going to enjoy this program and it is easy to use and simple to implement. I give you everything you need so sit back and go through this model slowly learning this technique carefully. Then do it!

Be sure to download the software module that works with this Applied Income Model workbook. Go here to download:

http://www.filefactory.com/file/c117d9e/n/AIM_Software.zip

Your Own Personal Bailout

Let's begin with a review of why you're here. On December 22, 2008, government agencies quietly made a controversial decision. The tabloids missed it; the whole thing was so hush-hush. Government intervention had just given everyday people like you and me the opportunity to quietly pocket piles of cash each Wednesday afternoon. That is, **IF those everyday people knew about this 'secret' and how to exploit it.**

A Gift from the Government...NOT!

First, I need to square something away with you because I know you're somewhat skeptical right now. We're conditioned to think that to get more money we have to work harder and smarter or both. It just doesn't seem right to make a couple of almost BLIND calls and receive checks. Where's the skill? Where are the blood, sweat and tears? I have to tell you that's precisely how I felt the first time I used the Applied Income Model.

Rest assured this is all 100% legal and we're NOT abusing the welfare system! Forget any (misguided) loyalty to politicians and start looking after number one.

Think for a minute how much more secure your life would be if you could effortlessly claim a check weekly using the program I will outline here for you.

Let's be ultra-conservative and call it just a grand ($1,000) a week or 4 grand a month.

Would $4,000 a month make a big change in YOUR life? I say it would! And it's not as if you have to give up your day job to claim these checks either.

We're LITERALLY talking about making 2-phone calls each week, blindly following simple steps like a robot. Can you handle that?

This money is virtually unconditional. It doesn't matter what happens in the world, stock markets or economies.

No more sweating about your income, mortgage payments or investments. And this isn't some long-winded plan you have to grow old waiting to take shape; it can happen straight away!

But I will tell you now, this window of opportunity is only open to you if can act quickly (more about this later).

So thanks for spending a few minutes with me - as you can see, it'll be well worth it. To explain more, I'll start at the beginning.

'Blank Checks'

When I learned about this low-profile government blunder, I looked for a way to exploit it for cold, hard INSTANT CASH. The government had practically written a heap of blank checks! Someone was going to make money from this. I just had to figure out an easy way of getting MY share. Ideally, all it would take is a couple of calls… just like promised in all those trading systems…then BAM! I had it! This government oversight was going to cause a lot of disruption in a certain marketplace. And 'disruption' (also known as "volatility") is all it takes to cash in from it. It doesn't matter about the outcome of this government-induced disruption, as long as there's disruption. Intrigued? So what was this strange government decision and how can you claim your cash from it?

Weekly Cash from a 24-Hour Window of Disruption

Before I explain further, let me strongly emphasize something: this is NOT one of those trading systems that recklessly gamble on a 50/50 chance! The reason I say this is because when I tell you what this proven money-pump revolves around, you might be inclined to think otherwise.

I'm not participating in the silly 'loser's game,' the game, where one person is betting against the other or where one person is selling a stock, currency or commodity and the other buying. Okay? Let me explain and please stay with me and remember that this is NOT a 50/50 chance trading system.

The price of something you use regularly is mostly affected by 2-government reports that are released each week. It used to be the case that these 2-reports both came out on a Wednesday morning. BUT the decision was made to change this schedule. Now, one of these reports comes out after the close of business on TUESDAY, while the other still comes out the next day (WEDNESDAY). So what?

Well, as I recently proved, this has created a period of extreme volatility in the price of this particular item. Each Tuesday night, through to the following Wednesday morning, the price of this item jumps around violently.

To make money from this fact I don't have to watch a computer screen every Tuesday night either - the whole thing is done automatically by placing one call on Tuesday and another the next day. Simple! It doesn't matter which way the price goes up or down. As long as there's significant volatility in the price, I make money.

Skimming the Establishment

I say: "let them mess around with complicated charts all day; let them sleep with a computer under their pillow; let them worry about the market turning against them." If you think about it, the whole trading thing is usually a GIANT guessing game playing 50/50 odds. Whether you're a professional or amateur, it all comes down to trying to guess which way a certain market will go - up or down.

It's time for another dark truth. Nobody knows anything for certain except privileged insiders and they will go to jail if they say or do anything to act on their knowledge (without declaring it). Near certain events is how real money is made, not playing with 50/50 odds. I only want to deal in relative certainties.

Preferably 'government-sponsored' ones! And don't worry; your check payments are made by a government-sanctioned organization. All 100% legit! So what's this item that has been affected by all the price disruption for those 24 hours? Let me explain further…

Cashing In

Okay, so what's this about exactly? What has the government done and how can you benefit? As we know from the Gulf Wars, with governments, it's always about OIL, or more specifically, the price of oil. Oil is power (quite literally!). Can you believe that in America, the popularity of the President moves opposite to the price of oil? That's to say, the world's most powerful man is only popular while the price of gas is low. Sad, but true! But it doesn't end there. You and I NEED oil and the government knows it. They use it as a wealth confiscation weapon against us in the form of heavily taxing gas at the pump.

Think about how much tax on gas you must have paid over the years! Wouldn't you like to get some of that back? In a roundabout way, that's what the government is letting you do; have a window of opportunity to get money from all their interference in oil prices. I've already explained that the APPLIED INCOME MODEL revolves around government-induced chaos in the price of something you use every day. That 'something' is oil. And not just through gas use; oil is used in the manufacturing of thousands of things, including plastics. Stay with me please, the background is worth understanding. Remember, we're talking about making a fast and easy grand or so a week for no more than a phone call and a click of a mouse.

Okay, so oil is critical and therefore, governments do all they can to affect the price of it. As you know, they'll even go to war over it. **Oil IS government politics.** As you may know, the price of anything on a free market (as oil is) is affected by the forces of supply and demand. You don't need me to tell you that the world is a fast-moving and hazardous place and this means the price of oil is forever up and down. There's an old joke about what a famous analyst said in response to a reporter's question once about what the market would do. He said: "It will fluctuate." Of course, though his answer was flippant, he was right. What's adding to violent fluctuations in the price of oil is the battle of extreme opinions.

One group argues that there is no more easily drilled oil and that therefore world oil production has 'peaked'. This is aptly called 'Peak-Oil Theory'. But an opposing group argues that the days of oil are numbered anyway as alternate and cleaner fuel sources come online. Plus, the deteriorating economic climate is set to reduce the usage of oil drastically. Both arguments have merit. Do I care who is right and who is wrong? No! As long as the tug of war continues!

To prove this point of the war of opinion raging about oil consider this: in just a few short months in early 2009, the price of oil went from around $30 a barrel to $70 a barrel without anything actually changing apart from peoples' opinions! So to recap: the price of oil is influenced by governments and it fluctuates a great deal. Now, here's why the APPLIED INCOME MODEL plan was born. As I explained in the invitation to get on board this plan, the price of oil is greatly influenced by 2-government reports that come out each week. The opportunity lies in the fact that just recently, the times these reports get released each week used to be the same, but now one of them got brought forward. **Don't worry about any of this! You won't be disseminating data or anything at all mundane!**

One government report comes from the Department of Energy (DOE). This comes out every Wednesday morning at 9:30 a.m. The other government report comes from The American Petroleum Institute (API). It comes out the day before (Tuesday) at 4:30 p.m.

From The Financial Times I quote: "Analysts said the early release of the API report was likely to bring additional volatility to the market as traders would use it for guidance for about 20-hours - particularly during Singapore and London trading - until the release of the official Department of Energy weekly report." So suffice to say, there will be significant movement in oil prices in this time window. So what?

So, this fact can make you more in a day than you currently earn in a MONTH! How? Glad you asked. Let me re-emphasize something first by saying we WON'T be sleeping with a computer under our pillow trying to figure out which way the price of oil is headed!

Obviously, it's one thing to know that prices will fluctuate wildly, but the million-dollar question is: WHICH WAY? Will the price go up or down?

Answer: "We don't CARE."

I don't like to play 50/50 games of chance. No, I like relative certainties, especially when they're government sponsored! What I'm going to show you is how to almost certainly make hundreds or even thousands (the choice is yours) every Wednesday thanks to this government policy. You will soon see how this really is practically 'free money from the government.' Before I go in-depth though, I'd like to make something crystal clear: The mechanism we'll be using to claim what I believe is effectively 'free money from the government' is simply that - only a MECHANISM. A means to an end!

Our checks won't be coming from Social Security. The mechanism we will use to get our hands on the cash is a financial broker - this is how we can take advantage of the government move. **RELAX: this is NOT a commodity trading system or anything complex.** Nor is it a foolish game of chance where we have to suffer a bunch of losers. All will be explained. Please stay with me…

So because we're not betting the price of oil will go a certain way and we're not playing silly gambling games of chance, I insist that this is not a trading system in the usual sense of the phrase. We are taking advantage of a government move by using a tool that offers a way to play off oil prices, that's it. Okay, so I need to explain more, but trust me, this is as simple as can be…

All you need to know and appreciate is that these fluctuations happen constantly in the price of oil and at certain times. **THE FLUCTUATIONS ARE BIG! Volatility is good!** And that's the key: BIG FLUCTUATIONS! Okay, hold that thought for a second while I explain the next part. With this type of tactic, you can 'bet' that the price of oil will rise and you can 'bet' that it will fall. Now, wouldn't it be great if you could do this: You make TWO bets: one bet that the price of oil will rise and another bet that the price of oil will fall. This is called a 'straddle'. **(I'm using the word 'bet' as an analogy - this is not a gambling system)**

In effect, both bets cancel each other out. So why bother? BECAUSE, one of those bets is going to emerge as a clear 'winner' in that window of time. We are simply going to bail out of the 'losing' bet and ride the winning one. One bet will take a small loss, but the other bet should cover that loss and make a profit on top. So what do we need to make this work then? **We need volatility.** Thanks to the government, we get it big time between 4:30 pm on a Tuesday and 9:30 am the next day.

You see, we don't care if the price of oil goes higher or lower, all we need is a large movement one way or the other to make this work. Let's put some color in this picture…

Let's say the price of oil this Tuesday at 4:30 is $51.00! This would be shown in cents and without the $ symbol or a decimal point, like so: "5100" This is effectively the price the broker has stated (in actuality, this is what the market is saying it is). You can place a bet on this number rising or falling; it's that simple. We are going to place a bet on BOTH a rise and a fall. TWO bets! When we see which bet is the winner, we dump the loser. That's it!

NOTE: This is also called a straddle because you are in effect straddling over the price – you could go in either direction. With a straddle if the move goes in your direction you should be able to make enough to offset the loss on your bet that it would not go in your direction, and with a **solid stop-loss** ("your built-in safety valve against loss")in place, you limit your downside while enjoying unlimited upside.

So I hope you're starting to see that we're not playing the usual silly game of betting/trading where we think we have a crystal ball and guess which way something is going. The government has caused price volatility and we can make money from them as a result. The mechanism of putting a double bet - a straddle trade - on with a financial broker is entirely incidental. We're not gamblers or traders in the usual sense. All will become very clear as we progress though the model but that's the essence of the APPLIED INCOME MODEL; the nearest thing to a sure thing I've ever seen and though we're using a trading platform to achieve our goal, we aren't sitting with the usual fools who play that game. Okay, enough with the theory, let's get on with it.

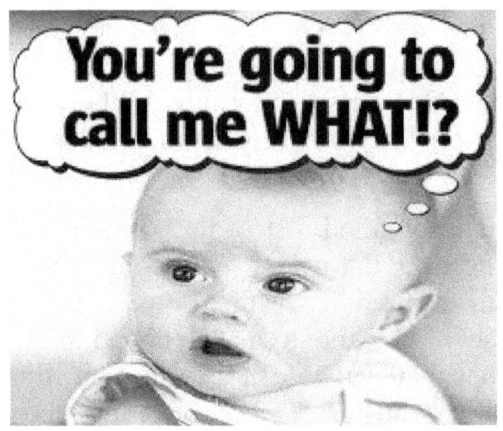

Things You'll Need

1. A phone with good reception: You'll be placing your trades with a phone. Ideally, you'd use a landline. All I can say is that you do NOT want to be out of contact once you have these 2-trades going on! Your cash can be made almost instantaneously. For those few minutes (sometimes less) it's all happening. Make sure at this time you have an uninterrupted connection.

2. A computer with high-speed Internet connection: You'll place the trade by phone but you'll be monitoring the action and closing the trade online. There's nothing complicated about this. No analyzing charts either! Like the phone, you must have total access for the short few minutes this will take. Make sure the computer is somewhere you can have peace and quiet too - that's why I prefer laptops - you can move positions to suit.

3. A Financial Brokerage account: We'll talk about this later (I even give you recommendations). You can be up and running instantly and do the whole thing online for free. I know some gambling systems require you to have multiple accounts to avoid any one broker closing you down. That doesn't apply in this case as the broker doesn't care how much money you make (more later on this).

4. Supporting Resources: More about this next; this is a deposit to trade on account with.

5. Records: We'll talk about this towards the end, but get hold of a notepad or a ledger. Nothing complicated, but we're going to keep a track on winnings. You'll find this handy later on when evaluating your past performances and to ensure you get all your winnings. There, nothing too demanding on that checklist I think you'll agree.

NOTE: Records are also important in order to file your income taxes properly. THERE IS NO WITHOLDING ON THESE PROFITS! I suggest you file a quarterly "estimate tax" (a bookkeeper or CPA can assist you with this filing). Be careful to file proper income taxes. This is very important!!!

Now let's talk about those supporting resources…

Supporting Resources

As you now know, The APPLIED INCOME MODEL doesn't rely on such a relatively hazardous system as playing the odds. If you're losing large amounts of money using this system then you're doing something VERY wrong! But having said that, I don't want you putting any more money on the table than you can afford to lose, especially in the early stages, just to be sure until you've got this system completely understood and function first by using practice trades before going "live". This section therefore involves looking at the worst case scenario and planning for it so we're never out of the game. Here's what you need to know to achieve that!

On each trade (we make 2-trades, remember) invest no more than "1-contract". In the next sections you'll learn what this means and how to apply it. Using this number each time and for both trades, each point (a point is one cent in the price of oil) traded is the equivalent of $10. So, if you get an oil price quote from the broker of 5100 and you buy it and it goes up to 5110, that means it is a 10 point move or the equivalent of $100 profit.

In the example shown, the 'FACTOR' you would use on each trade (you make 2-trades at a time, remember) would be $10. As you'll see, this number is not your total amount at stake. This figure is the amount you will claim per point (cent) of movement of the price of oil.

Don't worry, we'll be running some examples shortly. For now just understand that the rules are simple and strict: Do NOT deviate from your calculated factor! ONE CONTRACT per trade, each and every time without fail! Each of the two trades has the same factor (per point) as the others. No gut feelings or any superstitious nonsense; the same factor each time, no questions! Now, as and when you make money at this, you will have a choice to make:

1. Take the money you've made off the table and let the trade ride for 'free' (not a bad idea).

2. Increase the size of your factor with an accumulation of profits.

Now remember, your broker doesn't care how much money you make so the factor can keep getting higher and higher. The sky's the limit here. In theory, you could one day be making more in a few minutes than most people do in a year!!

Setting it Up!

So you need a broker to do this. We have some recommendations and it is quite simple to open an account.

Please note this is a listing for your convenience. We are not affiliated with these brokers in anyway. You may want to research other brokers to find one that best fits your needs.

5perside.com

http://www.5perside.com

1-800-523-7357

American Futures Trading

http://www.americanfuturestrading.com/tzpt

1-866-822-6872

Daniels Trading

http://www.danielstrading.com/triplezone

1-800-800-3840

1-312-706-7600

Foremost Trading LLC

http://www.TheFuturesBroker.com

1-888-262-6455

1-630-463-4510

James Mound Trading Group

http://www.moundreport.com

888-744-8866

1-386-447-6755

RMB Group

http://www.rmbgroup.com

1-800-345-7026

The steps are no different than opening a stock brokerage account. You will need to send in paperwork and an initial deposit for your margin account. And of course there are other alternatives for your options trading account. You can also try doing a Google search to find the brokerage or provider that's right for you.

The Claim Process

So where does the cash come from? It comes from people who are trading the opposite way to you. But of course, we are already effectively trading against ourselves aren't we? We're not playing the usual trading game. So don't worry about this. How does the broker make money then? They make it from something called the 'spread'. Let's turn to our recent oil price example.

Now just for the purposes of demonstration, forget the fact that we're placing 2-trades. Let's just say we're the average punter who wants to make a one-way trade; let's say that the price of oil will rise today. Your broker will go to the Index and he will get a quote for this first. This quote will be what the price of oil is trading at when he gets the quote. Let's say that the current price of oil is 5100 (by the way, this means in the real world it's $51.00 a barrel). Now, his quote won't be that though…

You know how when you change your currency to go abroad you see two figures; one figure for what you buy at and one figure for what you sell at? The foreign exchange agent makes their profit on the difference, right? Well, that's how the broker makes his money, only not with such exorbitant spreads as that airport currency exchange!

In this example that we are using for crude oil, the futures contracts trade every month of the year. In this trade, what we are going to be doing is buying one month and selling a different month. For example we might buy the

November Crude Oil Futures contract at say $51 and sell the December $51 contract at $51.50. **We will always be using two different months.** But, you have to remember that each contract is distinct and has its own price, and what we are trying to accomplish is to make money on a sharp move in one direction while cutting the loss on the losing side.

AND, THIS IS CRITICAL – FOR THE EXAMPLES WE ARE GIVING YOU FOR THE CRUDE OIL FUTURES YOU MUST USE TWO SEPARATE MONTHS FOR THE BUY AND THE SELL.

A typical quote for the price of oil on that day when we said it was 5100 then might be something like this "5095 and 5105" So the 'spread' is 5 points lower and higher of 5100- total spread of 10. Can you see that? That's how they get their cut and this is why they don't care how much money you make - what's it to them? As long as you're trading, they're making money! So what does that quote mean then?

It means that if you want to BUY oil (in other words you want to bet that the price of oil will rise) you can do so at 5105. If you want to sell oil, you can do so at 5095. If you want to SELL, you get the lower price. If you want to BUY, you get the higher price. Don't worry; we're not futures traders in the usual sense. This is just the terminology they use and you must learn the terminology as well as the rules. We're not buying anything or selling anything in the usual meanings of those words. Right, so let's turn back to the simple example we started with…

Just for demonstration purposes, we're not using the APPLIED INCOME MODEL here. We said that we are going to bet that the price of oil rises today. Great! So we get our quote from as: "5095 and 5105." So which of those two numbers quoted will be our buy price? Yep. The higher one: 5105. We place our trade by saying: "Buy at ten dollars a point." Ten dollars was our FACTOR, remember? The person on the other end of the phone confirms this and the trade is open. The broker takes some of your cash on deposit as a security and off we go...

Now let's say the trade goes in our favor and rises by 100 points. Great! We call to cash in. First, as before, we get a price. The broker then says: "5200 to 5210". Okay, if we opened this trade by 'buying', what terminology would we use to close this trade and cash in? We would do the opposite: 'sell'. Which price would we get - 5200 or 5210? The lower one: 5200. If you want to SELL, you get the lower price. If you want to BUY, you get the higher price. So the price for this trade was 5105 if you recall and the price when we closed this trade was 5200. We therefore gained 95 points (5200 minus 5105). We placed a factor (stake) per point of ten dollars so our profit then would be $950 (95 point gain multiplied by the factor per point of ten dollars).

Take a moment to perhaps re-read this section and get your head around it before moving on as we need to take another step to use this system correctly. You must first understand this example before we go further. Don't worry, when we run a few simulations you'll understand perfectly clearly.

Okay; so now you can see how this type of trade works, let's now look at how The APPLIED INCOME MODEL takes advantage of it.

In the example I just used, it was a one-way trade with a 50/50 chance, right? Either the price of oil was going to go up or down - 50/50! As previously mentioned, what we are going to do is place 2-EQUAL AND OPPOSITE TRADES. We are going to simultaneously BUY and SELL oil. When one trade emerges as a clear 'winner', we cut the 'loser' and ride the winner by closing each trade at an appropriate time. Make sense?

It's just like in that example before, only we're opening two trades not just that one, and the other trade is the exact opposite to the other. Same factor per point! Make sure you have your head around this before moving on!

Okay. We can automate the closing of the trade for the 'loser' by stating a point at which we want that trade to close. The language they use for this is a 'stop-loss'. Let's go back to our simplistic example for a second where we just had a single trade; we bet that the price of oil would rise if you recall as follows: we get our quote from the broker as: "5095 and 5105." So which of those two numbers quoted will be our buy price? Yep. The higher one: 5105. We place our trade by saying: **"Buy at ten dollars a point."** This much we already covered. But now we add something to our trade as follows: **"Buy oil at ten dollars a point AND a stop-loss at fifty points from entry."**

Here's what this means: we have now placed a trade that the price of oil will rise with a starting point of 5105. This we know from before. But NOW, we have an automated mechanism that will close this trade if it goes 50 points against us. So let's run that simulation.

We started with 5105 but if the price hits 5055 (5105 minus 50 points stop-loss set). Your broker closes this trade automatically. Now here's the thing: Both of our equal and opposite trades will have 50-point stop losses set at the opening. **This point is a key point!**

This mechanism is what will allow us to abandon the losing 'horse' in this race and ride the winner to profits to use a gambling analogy. Yes, one of our trades will be down 50 points, but the other trade should be up higher than that amount - enough to cover the broker's spread AND our loss on the other trade.

You can now perhaps see why we need big movements in the price to make money. The losing trade is strictly controlled and limited and the winning trade has unlimited upside. Now that's the sort of game I want to play!

If you're not excited at this point, it must be because you need to re-read this chapter. Please do so before continuing on to the next chapter.

Now think back to the chapter on the supporting resources where I explained to you the worst case scenario. The worst case scenario for The APPLIED INCOME MODEL is no big movement and instead the price wanders one way and activates the stop loss of one trade then wanders the other to activate the other stop loss. Now you can see why that might be very unlikely! But that's the safety system so please stick to it. If there is going to be a bad day it might be one where there's just very little movement at all and the trades cancel each other out. In this case the only loss would be the 'spread' the broker charges- a very nominal amount and again, this situation, while certainly not impossible, is unlikely and extremely unlikely to occur each and every day for sure.

Making the Calls

Okay so back to the magic call. It must be made as early as possible on a Tuesday evening - **any time from as early as 9pm EST and no later than 5am EST**. Why this time window? It is because of the Singapore trading time zone. The time between the 2-government reports being released is pretty much when London and Chicago trading pits are closed so not much volatility created from them, BUT in Asia, they are open from about 2am and 9am UK time).

As a recap: From The Financial Times I quote: "Analysts said the early release of the API report was likely to bring additional volatility to the market as traders would use it for guidance for about 20 hours - particularly during Singapore and London trading - until the release of the official Department of Energy weekly report."

Before making the call, have your computer on and connected to the Internet with your brokerage account logged in and ready to go. No interruptions!

Here's how the call might proceed thereafter:

You: "Hello. Account number X1234, name is Smith. Daily US Light Crude please!"

Broker: "Daily US Light Crude is 5095 and 5105."

You: I want to open two separate positions. I want to buy the November Crude oil future at 5105 and sell the December Crude Oil future at 5095.

The representative will then open each position one at a time and read them back to you. This needs to be done VERY quickly by the rep so don't stall him or ask any questions- just let him do what you said!

You (quickly and clearly): "I also want a stop-loss on EACH position 50 points from entry."

The rep repeats back and call ends. You are now watching your "Open Positions" screen and you should immediately see those two trades you put in appear. The first thing you'll notice on the right hand side is that the second the trades were placed they are both showing a small loss. Don't be concerned about this - that's just because of the brokers' spread and this is the cost of placing the trade. Things will change! Don't be surprised if one of the trades hits its stop-loss almost immediately or at least within minutes. Remember, this is automatic. As and when one of the trades does close automatically, you're now left with two things:

1. A loss from the losing trade. That money has already been taken from your money on deposit by the broker.

Forget about it now.

2. A remaining trade that will NOT close until you close it OR it hits the stop loss.

Your remaining trade needs to make up for the loss of the losing trade (50 points plus the cost of the trade). The second the winning trade is up 60 points you're in the money and you want it to stay that way. **You'll easily know if you're in the money by always remembering what 60 points is and comparing it to the profit now showing on the remaining trade on the right hand side.** BUT, this can quickly change so watch very closely as you pick up the phone and call the broker back:

You: "Account number X1234, name Smith. I want to place a trailing stop loss on my Daily US Light Crude open position activated at 60 points above open and trailing by 10 points."

Meanwhile, do NOT take your eye off the screen and let the remaining trade become a loser! What you've done now is ensured there is no loss in this trade AND unlimited upside. You can now sit back and watch it all happen automatically. The trade will now gather more and more cash if it continues to go in your favor. As and when it retreats by 10 points, your money is locked in.

Rehearsals

So now you're ready to start making some money! But start with some 'paper trades' using the provided Excel macro-software. By paper trades I mean pretending to make trade. Go through all the processes described, just don't actually open the trade. Here's what to do…

Phone the broker and get a quote just like in the real thing. Let's imagine they say 5095 and 5105. Enter this as shown in the top green boxes- the higher number of the quote goes in the blue "UP" box and the lower number of the quote goes in the red "DOWN" box:

You'll instantly see the software enter a lot of things automatically for you including the 50 point stop-loss levels and the buy and sell levels you entered already.

IMPORTANT: only write in the green boxes! Next, go to the section on the left hand side to enter your factor (previously calculated). Let's say this is 10 dollars:

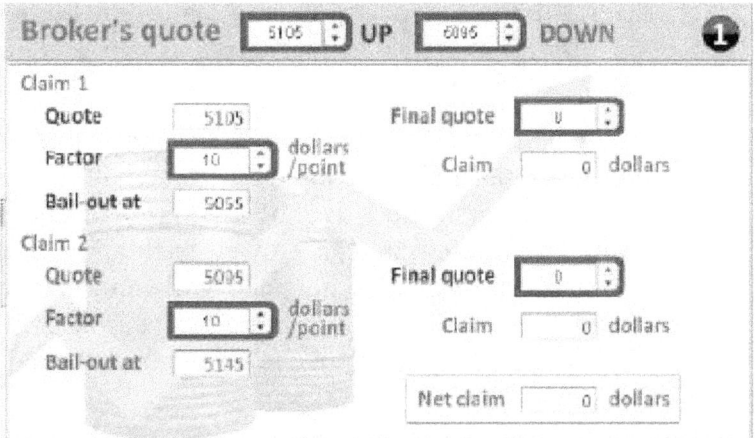

The two trades are color-coded. You'll see those colors reversed on the right hand side of this software when it comes to closing the trades because in order to close a BUY trade, you have to SELL and vice versa. Remember?

Okay. Now, to make this a realistic simulation you need to be doing this very fast so you don't miss any of the moves in the price that will start the very second you got that quote and entered it here.

So have a play around with this software for a bit first so you feel comfortable. Once you've entered the two quotes for Daily US Light Crude and your factor, watch the action closely using the dealing screen with your broker. Remember, this is just a simulation but this is the easiest way of seeing the two prices move without all the clutter.

So you have two trades to watch - red (sell) and blue (buy). The numbers to look for are the stop-losses the software automatically set for you. When the red stop-loss matches the red price on the screen, that trade is closed. Same for the blue one! Enter the number the trade closed at in the right hand side for the appropriate trade. Let's stick with our example and we'll say that the oil price went down 150 points thus, activating the stop-loss on our UP trade of 5055:

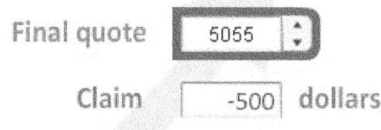

So that's the losing trade and it's now ditched with a loss of 500 dollars - this is calculated automatically by the software when you enter the number in the green box. You're now left with the remaining open trade- either red or blue. This is the part I really want you to practice before you do the real thing because this is the part that requires judgment on your part; up until now, it's been automated. You now have to decide when to cash in this winning trade. Remember, you're looking for at least a

33

60-point gain in this position to make both trades break even. Once that level is triggered, you can insert the automatic profit-lock I explained earlier. Okay, so let's now say that you close the winning trade at 4880. Enter this in the remaining box on the right hand side and now you'll see the cash made for both trades and the net trade calculated at the bottom: Your profit on this side of the trade is $2,150 for a net profit of $1,650.

Now let's look at what happens if the price moves up by $1.95 or 195 points: Your starting point is 5105 on the bet it is going up and 5095 on the bet it is going down. You have set your stop-loss as 50 points on each side.

As the price moves higher, you will be stopped out of the sell at 5145 (5095 plus 50 points). But, the buy side will remain open. As you can see in the slide, your loss on the sell transaction is $500 while your profit on the buy side is $1,950 for a net profit of $1,450.

So practice this a good few times first and run some simulations. That way the real thing will seem very simple indeed. However, don't put off the day of making an actual trade for too long because there is nothing better than actual experience.

When you see your own money in the balance, you will notice how your decision making steps up a gear or two! When you are 'paper trading' you are far more relaxed as you cannot mess up. And this is the reason that it is successful - when you are relaxed you make more sound judgments and aren't influenced by fear and greed. So when you do eventually start to trade, just relax and follow the rules.

By using this trading system with strict stop-losses and a volatile oil market which has easily shown moves of

$1.50 or more in the hours and days following the first report, you should be able to take all of your money off the table after 4 or 5-trades. Better still, you should be able to pull between $400 and $1,500 in spending money within hours or days of each reporting period. The key here is to make sure you have your stop-losses in effect because this market moves so fast, and to make sure that you are always risking the same amount on each side of the trade. And, if oil prices really move in one direction like $3 or $4, you will clean up on that trade.

Records

Keep records as you'll never know when you will need them. These are good for evaluating past performance and in the unlikely event any tax inspector asks where all this money came from you'll be able to show them. Your broker will send you a statement by email every time a trade is opened and/or closed so you'll have this too – be sure to print them off and file them. ALWAYS KEEP A PAPER-TRAIL! The easiest way to keep easy-to-follow records is to enter the numbers in the software every time you trade and print that off. If this isn't working for you for some reason on a continual basis, you're probably doing something wrong and your records are a good place to start figuring out why. Look at them and re-read this manual carefully! And again, don't use real money until you've run MANY simulations.

I Have a Special Gift for My Readers

I appreciate my readers for without them I am just another author attempting to make a difference. If my book has made a favorable impression please leave me an honest review. Thank you in advance for you participation.

My readers and I have in common a passion for the written word as well as the desire to learn and grow from books.

My special offer to you is a massive ebook library that I have compiled over the years. It contains hundreds of fiction and non-fiction ebooks in Adobe Acrobat PDF format as well as the Greek classics and old literary classics too.

In fact, this library is so massive to completely download the entire library will require over 5 GBs open on your desktop.

Use the link below and scan all of the ebooks in the library. You can select the ebooks you want individually or download the entire library.

The link below does not expire after a given time period so you are free to return for more books rather than clog your desktop. And feel free to give the link to your friends who enjoy reading too.

I thank you for reading my book and hope if you are pleased that you will leave me an honest review so that I can improve my work and or write books that appeal to your interests.

Okay, here is the link…

http://tinyurl.com/special-readers-promo

PS: If you wish to reach me personally for any reason you may simply write to mailto:support@epubwealth.com.

I answer all of my emails so rest assured I will respond.

Meet the Author

Dr. Leland Benton is Director of Applied Web Info, a holding company for ePubWealth.com, a leading ePublisher company based in Utah. With over 21,000 resellers in over 22-countries, ePubWealth.com is a leader in ePublishing, book promotion, and ebook marketing.

As the creator and author of "The ePubWealth Program," Leland teaches up-and-coming authors the ins-and-outs of today's ePublishing world. He has assisted hundreds of authors make it big in the ePublishing world.

Leland also created a series of external book promotion programs and teaches authors how to promote their books using external marketing sources.

Leland is also the Managing Director of Applied Mind Sciences, the company's mind research unit and Chief Forensics Investigator for the company's ForensicsNation unit. He is active in privacy rights through the company's PrivacyNations unit and is an expert in survival planning and disaster relief through the company's SurvivalNations unit.

Leland resides in Southern Utah.

Visit some of his websites
http://www.AddMeInNow.com
http://www.AppliedMindSciences.com
http://www.BookbuilderPLUS.com
http://www.BookJumping.com
http://www.EmailNations.com
http://www.EmbarrassingProblemsFix.com
http://www.ePubWealth.com
http://www.ForensicsNation.com
http://www.ForensicsNationStore.com
http://www.FreebiesNation.com
http://www.HealthFitnessWellnessNation.com
http://www.Neternatives.com
http://www.PrivacyNations.com
http://www.RetireWithoutMoney.org
http://www.SurvivalNations.com
http://www.TheBentonKitchen.com
http://www.Theolegions.org
http://www.VideoBookbuilder.com

Some Other Books You May Enjoy From ePubWealth.com, LLC Library Catalog

EPW Library Catalog Online
http://www.epubwealth.com/wp-content/uploads/2013/07/Leland-benton-private-turbo.pdf

EPW Library Catalog Download
http://www.filefactory.com/f/562ef3ea1a054f0a

www.ingramcontent.com/pod-product-compliance
Lightning Source LLC
Chambersburg PA
CBHW070720180526
45167CB00004B/1560